Copyright © Kids Lighthouse 2024
All rights reserved. No parts of this book may be copied, distributed, or published in any form without written permission from the publisher.

To:_____
   _____

From:_____
   _____

You are perfect just the way you are

ON ONE VERY SPECIAL DAY,
A BABY FOX WAS BORN.

ONE DAY, THE BABY FOX WAS SITTING WITH HIS MOM AND ASKED...

MOM, WHY DO I LOOK SO DIFFERENT?

I DON'T LOOK LIKE THE OTHER FOXES. I DON'T WANT TO BE DIFFERENT.

MOM FOX LOOK SURPRISED AND SADDENED.

THEN WITH A SMILE
SHE SAID...

BABY FOX, DON'T YOU REALIZE THAT BEING DIFFERENT IS WHAT MAKES YOU SO SPECIAL?

As Mom Fox held Baby Fox closer, she started to tell him a story.

SOMETIMES, YOU MAY THINK THAT BEING DIFFERENT IS A BAD THING...

BUT, IF YOU CHOOSE TO
LOOK AT LIFE
DIFFERENTLY, IT CAN
BE A GOOD THING.

BABY FOX PERKED HIS EARS TO LISTEN CLOSER.

MOM FOX CONTINUED.

MOM FOX THEN ASKED
BABY FOX THIS...

IF A BUTTERFLY WAS MISSING PART OF IT'S WING, WOULD IT MAKE IT UGLY?

OF COURSE NOT, SAID BABY FOX. I LOVE BUTTERFLIES!

MOM FOX THEN ASKED
BABY FOX...

WHAT IF A LIZARD WAS PURPLE INSTEAD OF BROWN? WOULD YOU THINK IT WAS UGLY?

No way, said Baby Fox. It would be so cool!

THEN MOM FOX ASKED...

WHAT IF A POLAR BEAR HAD BLUE AND WHITE FUR? WOULD YOU THINK IT WAS UGLY?

BABY FOX WAS SO EXCITED. HE REPLIED, DO THOSE EXIST? THAT WOULD BE SO AWESOME!

MOM FOX THEN SAID...

WHAT ABOUT A COLORFUL BIRD? WOULD THE BIRD BE LESS SPECIAL?

No way! replied Baby Fox. It would be super special!

LOOKING AT BABY FOX WITH SO MUCH LOVE IN HER HEART REPLIED...

IF YOU TRULY BELIEVE THAT A BUTTERFLY WITHOUT PART OF IT'S WING IS SPECIAL...

AND A PURPLE LIZARD IS COOL...

AND A BLUE AND WHITE
POLAR BEAR IS AWESOME...

AND A COLORFUL BIRD IS SPECIAL...

THEN WHY IS IT SO HARD TO BELIEVE THAT YOUR DIFFERENCE IS WHAT MAKES YOU SO SPECIAL?

HMM, SAID BABY FOX. I NEVER THOUGHT ABOUT IT THAT WAY.

Mom Fox replied, did you know that God created you in his own image?

So God created man in his own image; in the image of God he created him; male and female he created them.

Genesis 1:27

FROM YOUR HEAD DOWN TO YOUR LITTLE TOES, HE CREATED YOU.

AFTER GOD CREATED MAN AND ANIMALS, GOD CALLED HIS CREATION GOOD.

"THEN GOD SAW EVERYTHING THAT HE HAD MADE, AND INDEED IT WAS VERY GOOD."

GENESIS 1:31

YOU ARE PART OF GOD'S CREATION, THEREFORE, GOD SEES YOU AS GOOD.

HE LOVES YOU JUST
THE WAY YOU ARE.

HE EVEN LOVES THE THINGS THAT MAKE YOU DIFFERENT.

JUST LIKE YOU LOVE THE BUTTERFLY, LIZARD, POLAR BEAR, AND BIRD.

BUT MOM, THE BABY FOX REPLIED, WHY DID GOD MAKE ME DIFFERENT?

WELL, SAID MOM FOX, GOD MADE YOU DIFFERENT, BECAUSE IN GOD'S EYES, YOUR DIFFERENCE IS BEAUTIFUL.

GOD LOOKS AT YOU AND HE SEES HIS LOVE FOR YOU.

HE ALSO SEES BEAUTY IN THE THINGS THAT MAKE YOU DIFFERENT.

JUST LIKE YOU SEE A COLORFUL BIRD AND THINK IT'S SPECIAL.

BABY FOX ASKED, SO GOD LOVES THAT I'M DIFFERENT?

YES, SAID MOM FOX.

GOD LOVES YOU JUST THE WAY YOU ARE.

THE BABY FOX REPLIED, MOM, DO YOU LOVE ME THE WAY THAT I AM?

MOM FOX SMILED AND REPLIED, ALWAYS.

Always Remember that being different is what makes you so special!

To see more books by
Kids Lighthouse, please visit
KidsLighthouse.com

www.ingramcontent.com/pod-product-compliance
Lightning Source LLC
Chambersburg PA
CBRC090837010526
44118CB00007B/235